John Cabot
Early Explorer

Wendy Mass

Enslow Publishers, Inc.

40 Industrial Road	PO Box 38
Box 398	Aldershot
Berkeley Heights, NJ 07922	Hants GU12 6BP
USA	UK

http://www.enslow.com

Library of Congress Cataloging-in-Publication Data

Mass, Wendy, 1967–
    John Cabot : early explorer / Wendy Mass.
       p. cm. — (Explorers!)
    Summary: Discusses the life of John Cabot, with an emphasis on his
career as an early explorer of North America.
    Includes bibliographical references (p.) and index.
    ISBN 0-7660-2144-0
    1. Cabot, John, d. 1498?—Juvenile literature. 2. America—Discovery
and exploration—English—Juvenile literature. 3. North
America—Discovery and exploration—English—Juvenile literature.
4. Explorers—North America—Biography—Juvenile literature.
5. Explorers—Great Britain—Biography—Juvenile literature.
6. Explorers—Italy—Biography—Juvenile literature. [1. Cabot, John,
d. 1498? 2. Explorers. 3. America—Discovery and exploration—English.]
I. Title. II. Explorers! (Enslow Publishers)
E129.C1M37 2004
808'.042'071073—dc21

                    2002155207

Printed in the United States of America

10 9 8 7 6 5 4 3 2 1

To Our Readers: We have done our best to make sure all Internet Addresses in this book were active and appropriate when we went to press. However, the author and the publisher have no control over and assume no liability for the material available on those Internet sites or on other Web sites they may link to. Any comments or suggestions can be sent by e-mail to comments@enslow.com or to the address on the back cover.

Every effort has been made to locate all copyright holders of material used in this book. If any errors or omissions have occurred, corrections will be made in future editions of this book.

Illustration Credits: © 1996-2003 ArtToday.com, Inc., pp. 7, 14, 21, 22 (inset), 24 (inset), 28, 31, 42 (inset); © 1999 Artville, LLC., pp. 4, 6, 16, 19, 29, 34; Corel Corporation, pp. 8, 11, 24 (background), 26, 36, 41; Enslow Publishers, Inc., p. 32; Library of Congress, pp. 1, 10, 12, 14, 18, 20, 22 (background), 25, 30, 37, 39, 40.

Cover Illustration: background, Monster Zero Media; portrait, Library of Congress.

Please note: Compasses on the cover and in the book are from © 1999 Artville, LLC.

Contents

John Cabot was born in Italy. Years later he moved to Spain with his wife and children. When Cabot was ready to explore, he needed someone to pay for his trip. So he moved to England and sailed for the king of England.

Why Is John Cabot Famous?

An explorer is a person who travels in search of new places. Six hundred years ago, the people of Europe wanted to find a way to get to China, Japan, and India. These countries were known as the Indies. Gold, jewels, spices, and silk came from there.

One Italian explorer became very famous. His name was Christopher Columbus. We know all about his adventures and the land he discovered. John Cabot was also an Italian explorer. He crossed the same ocean and had the same dreams. But we hardly know anything about him. No one knows exactly when or where he was

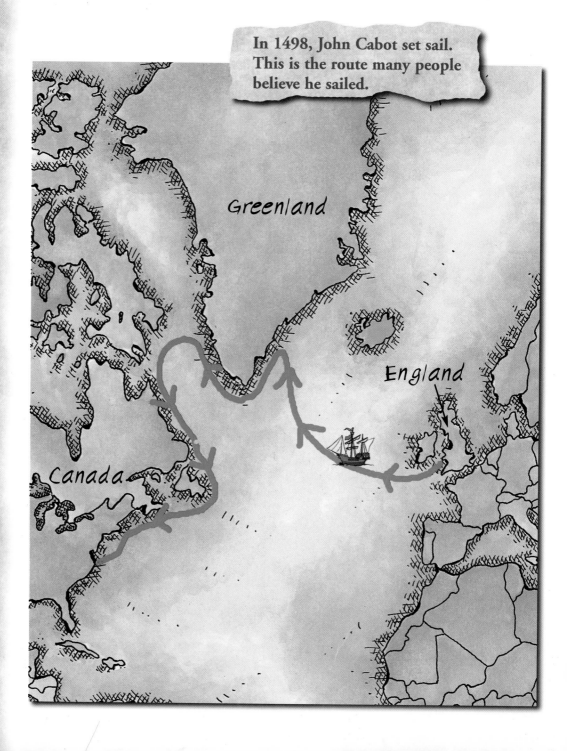

In 1498, John Cabot set sail. This is the route many people believe he sailed.

Greenland

England

Canada

born, exactly where he grew up, or what he looked like. Even his death is a big mystery.

What we do know is that he lived a very exciting life and made many important discoveries.

John Cabot and his son Sebastian discovered new lands.

When John Cabot was a boy, his family moved to Venice, Italy. St. Mark's Square (above) and the Rialto Bridge (below) are in Venice.

Cabot's Early Years

John Cabot was born in Genoa, Italy. He was born about 1450. No one wrote down the year he was born. His name in Italian was Giovanni Caboto. His father was a merchant. John had one brother named Piero.

When John was a boy, the family moved to Venice, Italy. Venice was a very important and busy place at that time. Traders sailed to faraway places. They would bring back spices and silk. They would then sell these goods at very high prices. Every few weeks, ships returned to Venice with chests full of items from faraway lands.

In Venice, John Cabot saw many ships and the goods that the ships brought from faraway places.

Treasures of the Indies

The countries of China, Japan, India, and the East Indies were known by one name. People in Europe called the whole area the Indies. There was a route to Europe from the Indies. Goods, like spices and silk, were brought by boat across the Red Sea. Then the goods were loaded onto camels and taken across land to the Mediterranean Sea. The goods were loaded onto ships sailing to

"Judith" by Lucas Cranach the Elder

Many people wanted to wear fancy clothes made out of silk that merchants brought back from China.

"Portrait of a Young Man" by Il Bronzino

Europe. The route was dangerous. Traders from Europe were not welcomed on the land route. So, people wanted to find an all-water route to the Indies.

People of long ago did not have refrigerators to keep food from going bad. They used spices like pepper, cloves, cinnamon, and nutmeg to cover up the taste of spoiled food. These spices could be found in the Indies.

Kings, queens, and other rich people of long ago loved to dress in fancy silk clothes. Only the people of China knew how to make silk. They did not share their secret of making silk with people of other countries.

Anyone who could find a new route to the Indies

Marco Polo was another famous explorer. He went to China.

would become very rich. Several tries were made to go around Africa. But none had worked. Ships were not very strong, and many ships were lost at sea.

New Adventures

John Cabot grew up hearing sailors talk about their adventures. The men talked about lands filled with riches. John also heard tales of Marco Polo's two visits

Marco Polo (1254–around 1324)

Marco Polo was born in Venice, Italy. At seventeen years old, Polo traveled for over three years to reach China. While there, he was sent on many official trips by the Mongol ruler of China, Kublai Khan. After twenty-four years in China, Polo returned to his home. He told of his adventures in Asia and China to a writer. Polo's book, *Description of the World*, told people of Europe about Chinese customs. It might have even inspired many people to explore.

to China. He wanted his own adventure. He wanted to sail on the seas.

Cabot started as a crewman on other men's ships. He learned how to use a compass. This tool told the captain which direction the boat was heading. Cabot also made maps, charts, and globes. Soon he was captain of his own ship. Cabot made many trips in and out of the ports of Venice. A port is a part of a town where ships can dock

John Cabot started out as a crewman on other ships. Soon he was captain of his own ship. He made many trips in and out of the ports of Venice.

to load or unload goods. Soon after, he married a woman named Mattea. The couple might have had daughters as well as sons. But only the names of the boys are known. Their names were Ludovico (known as Lewis), Sebastiano (Sebastian), and Sancio. When the children were still young, the family moved to Valencia, Spain. Cabot wanted to build a port there, but never did. Greater things were ahead for him.

Around 1494, John Cabot moved his family to Bristol, England. He would start his trip from there.

Getting Ready to Sail

England, Spain, Portugal, and France were tired of not being able to safely trade in the Indies. By studying maps and listening to traders, Cabot came up with a plan. He thought he could reach the Indies by going west across the Atlantic Ocean. Christopher Columbus had thought the same thing but planned on going south. According to Cabot, the fastest route would be if he sailed north.

Columbus set off south in 1492 and returned the next year. He brought back animals, like parrots. He brought back gold and jewels. Most people thought he had reached the Indies, but some did not think so. The land

Christopher Columbus discovered new lands as he was trying to find the Indies.

Christopher Columbus (1451–1506)

Christopher Columbus was born in Genoa, Italy. Like many explorers of his time, he wanted to find an all-water route to the Indies. Columbus sailed west. He landed on islands in the Caribbean Sea, which he thought were the Indies. Columbus went on four trips between 1492 and 1504. During these trips, he explored what are today called the West Indies and the coasts of Central and South America.

he talked about did not sound like the Indies that Cabot knew. He also did not think that Columbus had gone far enough west to have reached the Indies.

When news of Columbus's discovery reached Europe in 1493, Cabot knew he had to act fast. He wanted to show that his route would be the best. First, he needed money to pay for the trip. The rulers of Spain were already paying for Columbus's trip. Around 1494, Cabot moved his family to Bristol, England. Bristol was the

During this time, many people were searching for the Indies, which they believed to be China, Japan, and India. This is how they look today.

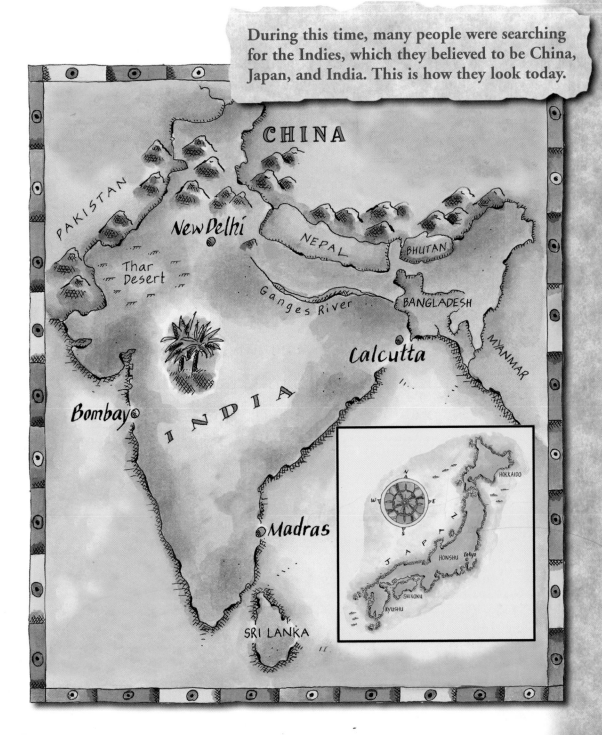

King Henry VII gave Cabot permission to sail on March 5, 1496.

second most important and richest port in England. Cabot knew the Bristol traders wanted to make their trade routes bigger. The Bristol sailors might have already traveled west on the Atlantic.

Cabot quickly became friends with the traders there. They gave him money. He changed his name from Giovanni Caboto to John Cabot, which sounded more like an English name. He went to London and met with King Henry VII. The king liked Cabot's idea and gave him his approval. A patent giving permission to sail was given to Cabot on March 5, 1496. The patent said that Cabot could sail east, west, and north on the Atlantic.

The patent did not give Cabot the right to explore the southern seas. The southern seas were under the control of Columbus and the Spanish government. Columbus wanted to teach people about Christianity. Cabot only wanted to find goods to buy and trade. This was just fine with the king. He left all the planning of the trip to Cabot. Having the support of the king meant that Cabot was finally able to follow his dream.

John Cabot left Bristol, England, ready to explore new lands.

John Cabot and his men landed in southeast Canada. The men on the ship had to look out for icebergs and polar bears (lower right).

Across the Atlantic

John Cabot was so excited that he tried sailing across the Atlantic only a few months later. But he had to turn back because he was running out of food. He was also having problems with the crew. He planned more carefully for the next trip. King Henry VII let him have only one ship, which Cabot named the *Matthew*. It was less than seventy feet long and had three masts. Cabot had a crew of eighteen men.

The ship was stocked with dried and salted fish, dried peas, dried and salted strips of beef, biscuits, flour, and beer. There would not be anywhere along the way to stop for food. The *Matthew* set sail from Bristol Harbor near the end of May 1497. Cabot's son Sebastian would have been a teenager by this time and may have gone on the voyage.

Ships of the time looked like this. The *Matthew* (inset) was recreated in 1997.

After leaving port, the ship rounded Ireland and headed north for a few days before turning west. Sailing the choppy North Atlantic Ocean was hard. Even though it was summer, they were so far north that the air was very cold and foggy. The smallest wave bounced the ship up and down. Water spilled onto the deck and had to be pumped off the ship. With eighteen men, the ship was also very cramped.

The person who looked out for icebergs and large rocks had one of the most important jobs on the ship.

There were no machines or computers to tell the captain if the ship was on course or to measure its speed. Cabot had to judge the position of the ship by looking at the sun or a bright star. There were no weather forecasts to warn the crew of upcoming storms.

The exact route that Cabot took is now lost to history. Cabot took notes and drew maps, but they no longer exist. It is believed that the *Matthew* traveled between thirty days and six weeks before it found land on June 24, 1497.

As Cabot's ship sailed, they ran into cold weather and fog.

No one really knows where John Cabot landed. Some think it was Newfoundland, Canada. Others think it might have been Nova Scotia, Canada.

Newfoundland, Canada

Nova Scotia, Canada

5

Finding New Lands

But where did the ship land? Some people believe it was most likely Newfoundland, Cape Breton Island, Labrador, or Nova Scotia. All of these places are in southeast Canada. One story says Cabot named the land "Prima Tierra Vista," which means "New Found Land." That is why that part of Canada is called Newfoundland today. Cabot thought he had found an island in Asia.

The first thing Cabot's sailors noticed was all the fish. The sea was filled with more fish than they had ever seen. Cabot said he could lower a weighted bucket, and it would fill up with fish. This was a big discovery because

Newfoundland

John Cabot, in 1497, may have landed on the island that is today called Newfoundland. It became a part of Canada in 1949. St. John's is the capital of Newfoundland. Most of the people there live near the sea. Fishing is a very big industry. But, with so many people fishing, the government had to stop people from fishing for cod and other types of fish. Today, the main catch is shellfish such as crab and lobster.

When Cabot arrived off the coast of Newfoundland, he found the waters were full of fish called cod.

fish was a big part of the European diet. This meant that the sailors from Bristol could return to this area and bring fish back with them to England. It also meant that the crew of the *Matthew* would have some fresh food to eat.

Cabot anchored the ship offshore. He and a few men took a small boat and sailed toward the land. When they landed on the shore, Cabot stuck two flags in the ground. One was the flag

All the places that people think Cabot landed are in southeast Canada.

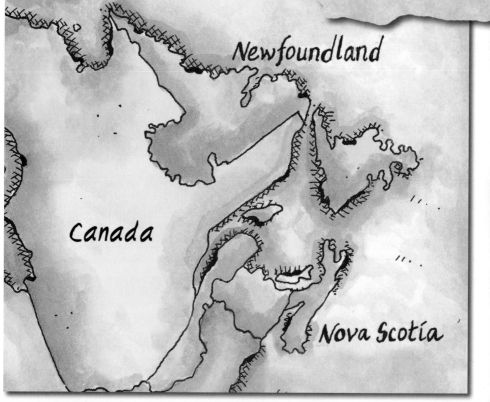

Newfoundland

Canada

Nova Scotia

of King Henry VII, and the other was of St. Mark, the patron saint of Venice.

Cabot and his men explored the area, never going too far from the shore. They did not want to risk being attacked by anyone who might live there. They wanted to make sure they returned home safely to report their discoveries. The men looked around this strange, new land. They found a trail and a site where a fire had been made. They also found a carved, painted stick and traps to catch animals. They even saw fields that looked like they had been cleared for villages. But they did not see any people or houses. They brought the stick back to the *Matthew* with them. They continued exploring the coast from the ship.

When Cabot claimed the land for England, he also planted a flag in the ground for St. Mark, who was the patron saint of Venice.

The ship traveled along the coast for about a month. Cabot never went ashore again. At one point, the sailors saw two running figures. The sailors were too far away to tell if the figures were animals or humans. By this time, their food was running out and spoiling. Cabot turned the ship around and headed back to England. The wind came up from behind the ship, helping it to go faster. Cabot might have made it back home in only fifteen days. He arrived on August 6, 1497. A few days later he met with the king.

When Cabot and his men were finished exploring the island they found, they sailed their ship down the coast for a month.

After Cabot returned to England, Henry VII gave him money and more boats so he could go back to the land that he had discovered.

6

What Happened to John Cabot?

John Cabot told King Henry VII about his trip. He told all about the land and all the fish. He did not find any spices or jewels. He was sure that he just needed to keep looking. By planting the flag of England, Cabot had claimed the new land for the English people. A hundred years later, the English would begin to move to America. King Henry VII was very pleased with Cabot's report. He gave him a gift of ten pounds, which today would be around $6,000. He also promised Cabot that he would receive twenty pounds a year.

Cabot quickly planned a second voyage. He hoped

that this time he would find Japan. His plan was to land in the same place he did on his first trip. Then he would follow the coast southwest until he reached Japan. In the spring of 1498, Cabot once again sailed out of Bristol Harbor. This time he had five ships, about

John Cabot sailed west from England. After a stop in Ireland, he crossed the Atlantic Ocean. He was hoping to find China, Japan, and India. Instead he found North America. He might have even landed in the Bahamas. No one knows for sure.

two hundred men, and objects like lace and cloth to trade. It is not known if the *Matthew* was one of the ships used for this trip as well. Between them, the five ships had enough supplies to last for a year. Some of the men planned to stay and set up a trading post in the distant land. Local merchants and even a few priests went along.

Soon after setting sail, one ship had to land in Ireland to be repaired. This is where the story of John Cabot ends. He and the other four ships were never heard from again. Were they lost at sea in a storm? Were they attacked? There are three clues that tell us what may have happened.

First, there is a map of America made in 1500 by Juan de la Cosa, a Spanish sailor and mapmaker. Cosa sailed with Christopher Columbus in 1492. On the map are drawings of five little English flags down the east coast. There was also a note on the maps that said, "Sea discovered by the English." This may have meant that at least some of the four ships made it to America. They

It was not long after leaving Bristol that Cabot and his men ran into trouble. One of the ships had to land in Ireland for repairs.

might have sailed along the coastline, claiming it for England.

Then in 1501, explorers found a piece of an Italian sword and Venetian earrings belonging to an American Indian. Did the objects wash ashore from a shipwreck? Did one of the ships reach the shore? Did the sailors trade with the American Indians before traveling on?

Did Cabot and his men become shipwrecked? Or lose a fight and die in the new lands? No one knows for certain.

Did Cabot and his men lose a fight and die there? Nobody knows the answer. But the fact that the objects were found might mean that at least one of the ships made it across the ocean.

Last, in 1501, a Spanish explorer wrote of meeting an English ship in the Bahamas. Was this Cabot and his men? At this time, that area was protected by the Spanish. If the report is true, it is likely the English sailors would not have been able to leave safely.

Both Columbus and Cabot died believing they had reached the Indies. They did not know North America was in between. They also believed the earth was smaller than it is. So the Indies were actually much further away than they had thought. A few years after Cabot's discovery, the English began to realize that the new land was an undiscovered place.

When Cabot did not return to England after his 1498 trip, his son Sebastian took his place. He sailed across the ocean in search of riches. He even said that he was the one who had discovered North America in 1497. It was

Sebastian Cabot (around 1484–1557)

Sebastian Cabot was John Cabot's second son. He was born in Venice, Italy. Sebastian became a mapmaker and a navigator. He may have sailed with his father on his first North American voyage in 1497.

Sebastian was also an explorer and tried to find the Northwest Passage. Explorers at this time thought there was a waterway to the Indies through North America. Sebastian Cabot thought he had found the passage during one of his trips, but his crew did not want to continue.

Sebastian Cabot was always looking for ways to get rich. He would sail for any country that would give him money to go on trips. That made him unpopular with many countries.

People believe Sebastian Cabot died around 1557.

After John Cabot did not return to England, Sebastian Cabot sailed across the ocean to discover more land for England.

not until the 1800s that historians found out John Cabot was the one who discovered North America.

For the 500th anniversary of Cabot's 1497 voyage, a copy of the *Matthew* was built in England. It was built in

John Cabot and Sebastian went ashore to explore the new lands.

Many can do their own exploring on the Cabot Trail in Nova Scotia, Canada.

Bristol Harbor, near where the original would have been built. The new *Matthew* sailed to Newfoundland in 1997, where there was a big celebration. The ship is now docked back in Bristol, where it reminds the world of John Cabot's great voyage of discovery.

Timeline

1450—John Cabot is born in Genoa, Italy.

1461—Moves to Venice, Italy.

late 1470s-mid-1480s—Marries a woman named Mattea and has three sons, Lewis, Sebastian, and Sancio.

1480s—Moves to Spain for a few years.

1494—Moves to Bristol, England.

1496—Tries to sail west to Asia, but is forced to return to England.

1497—Sets sail on the *Matthew* and reaches some part of Canada.

1498—Sets out once again, this time with five ships. He is never heard from again.

1997—The recreation of the *Matthew* sails to Newfoundland, Canada.

Words to Know

compass—A device that uses a magnetic needle to show direction.

explorer—A person who travels in search of new places.

merchant—A storekeeper.

patent—Permission from an authority, such as a king, to act on an idea.

port—An area of a town where ships can dock to load or unload goods.

pounds—A unit of money used in England, Ireland, Scotland, and other countries.

trader—Someone who buys and sells goods for money.

Venetian—Someone who is from the city of Venice.

Learn More About
John Cabot

Books

Champion, Neil. *John Cabot*. Chicago: Heinemann Library, 2001.

January, Brendan. *Explorers of North America*. New York: Children's Press, 2000.

Mattern, Joanne. *The Travels of John and Sebastian Cabot*. Austin, Tex.: Steadwell Books, 2001.

Shields, Charles J. *John Cabot and the Rediscovery of North America*. Philadelphia: Chelsea House, 2002.

Learn More About
John Cabot

Internet Addresses

John Cabot

<http://www.heritage.nf.ca/exploration/cabot.html>

Learn more about John Cabot and his adventures.

The *Matthew* of Bristol

<http://www.matthew.co.uk/>

See the Matthew, *John Cabot's ship.*

Index